HOW HAPPILY SHE LAUGHS

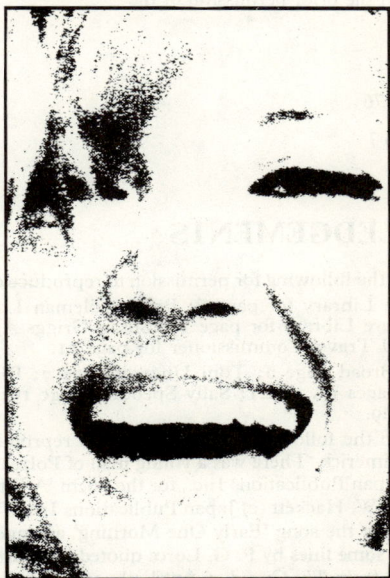

IAN SERRAILLIER

Longman
1724-1974

GW01465736

Longman Group Limited
London

*Associated companies, branches and representatives
throughout the world*

© Ian Serraillier 1976

First published 1976

ISBN 0 582 53846 7

ACKNOWLEDGEMENTS

We are grateful to the following for permission to reproduce copyright photographs:
Barnaby's Picture Library for page 8; Bruce Coleman Ltd., for pages 16 & 17;
Mary Evans Picture Library for page 10; Susan Griggs Agency for pages 4 & 5;
The New Zealand Travel Commissioner for page 11.
Artists: Linda Broad page 6; Toni Ungerer page 7; Richard Yeend page 14;
Graham Round pages 15, 20, 21; Sally Spedding page 19; Raymond Briggs page
27; Ffolkes page 29.
We are grateful to the following for permission to reproduce copyright material:
The author for a limerick 'There was a young man of Polzeath' by Nicholas Burns;
The author and Japan Publications Inc., for the poem 'A Bitter Morning' from *The
Way of Haiku* by J.W. Hackett (c) Japan Publications Inc. Tokyo; The Daily News
Ltd for the music of the song 'Early One Morning' arranged by H.A. Chambers;
The Guardian for some lines by F. G. Lorca quoted in an article entitled 'Lorca' by
Nicholas de Jongh from *The Guardian* April 4th, 1973; Oxford University Press for
the poem 'Too Polite' from *Happily Ever After* by Ian Serraillier, published by
Oxford University Press; Penguin Books Ltd for the extract 'There is Nothing That
is Not Spirit' from *The Upanishads* translated by Juan Mascaro (c) Juan Mascaro
1965. We regret we have been unable to trace the copyright holders of the following
material: The poem 'The Old Pig Whistles' by Richard Chase from *American
Folk Tales and Songs*.

Filmset in Hong Kong by
T.P. Graphic Arts Services
Printed in Hong Kong by
Yu Luen Offset Printing Factory Ltd.

CONTENTS

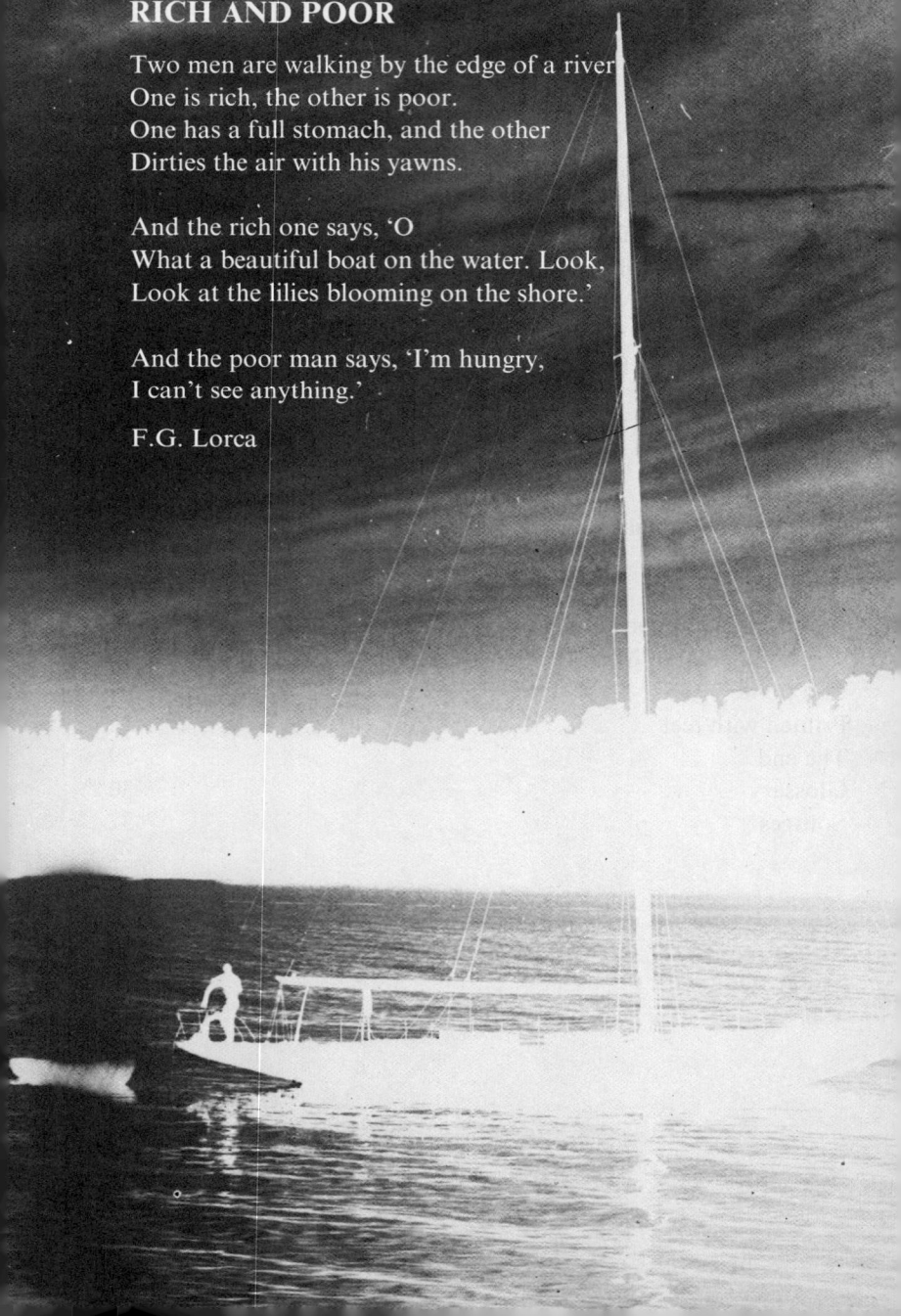

RICH AND POOR

Two men are walking by the edge of a river
One is rich, the other is poor.
One has a full stomach, and the other
Dirties the air with his yawns.

And the rich one says, 'O
What a beautiful boat on the water. Look,
Look at the lilies blooming on the shore.'

And the poor man says, 'I'm hungry,
I can't see anything.'

F.G. Lorca

HOW CATS BEGAN

Said Noah, 'Those rats and mice,
O dear! I thought them nice.
But they eat our food, both bad
And good, and drive me mad.
    O help me, God!
    O help me, God!'

Said God, 'You're hard to please.'
He told the Lion to sneeze.
It sneezed—sneezed out two cats,
That caught the mice and rats.
    'O thank you, God!
    O thank you, God!'

WILLIE PUSHED HIS SISTER NELL

Willie pushed his sister Nell
Down the family drinking well.
She's there yet, because it killed her—
Now we have to buy a filter.

YOUNG SAMMY WATKINS JUMPED OUT OF BED

Young Sammy Watkins jumped out of bed;
He ran to his sister and cut off her head.
This gave his mother a great deal of pain;
She hopes he will never do it again.

WILLIE WITH A THIRST FOR GORE

Willie, with a thirst for gore,
Nailed his sister to the door.
Mother, coming in, turned faint:
'Willie, Willie, mind the paint!'

SIX DUKES WENT A-FISHING

Six dukes went a-fishing
Down by the seaside.
One of them saw a dead body
Washed up by the tide.

The one spoke to the other,
These words I heard him say:
'It's the Royal Duke of Grantham
That the tide has washed away.'

They took him up to Portsmouth,
To a place where he was known;
From there up to London,
To the place where he was born.

They laid out his body
And stretched out his feet;
They covered him with flowers,
With roses so sweet.

Six dukes stood in front,
Twelve raised him from the ground,
Nine lords followed after him
Through the weeping town.

Black were their long coats,
Their walking sticks were white,
And each carried in his hand
A yellow burning light.

They laid him between two towers,
They laid him in cold clay;
And the Royal Queen of Grantham
Went weeping away.

EARLY ONE MORNING

Early one morning, just as the sun was rising,
I heard a maid sing in the valley below,
    'O, don't deceive me!
    O, never leave me!
How could you use a poor maiden so?

'Remember the promises you made to your Mary;
Remember the garden where you promised to be true.
    O, don't deceive me! *etc*

'O, gay is the garland, and fresh are the roses,
I've picked from the garden to bind on your brow.
    O, don't deceive me!' *etc.*

Thus sang the poor maiden, her tears sadly falling;
Thus sang the poor maiden in the valley below.
    'O, don't deceive me!' *etc.*

English Air
Arr. by H.A.C.

9

WEATHER

Evening red and morning grey
Send the traveller on his way;
Evening grey and morning red
Bring the rain upon his head.

When the wind is in the east,
It's good for neither man nor beast;
When the wind is in the north,
The fisherman he goes not forth;
When the wind is in the south,
It blows the bait in the fishes' mouth;
When the wind is in the west,
Then it's at the very best.

When the dew is on the grass,
Rain will never come to pass.

Red sky at night,
Shepherd's delight;
Red sky in the morning,
Shepherd's warning.

When clouds appear
   Like rocks and towers,
The earth's refreshed
   By frequent showers.

Rain, rain, go away,
Come again another day—
Not a public holiday!

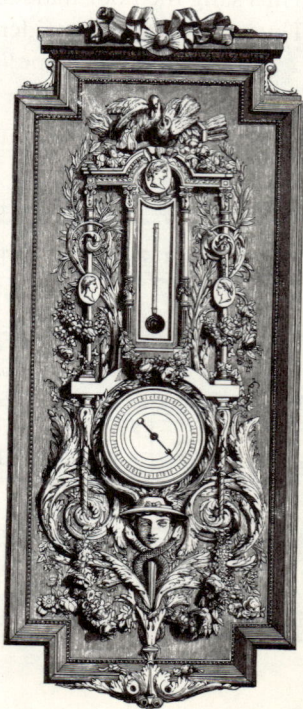

ON TRAVELLING FROM ENGLAND TO NEW ZEALAND

The waiters don't understand
English; and we can't speak
Portuguese. We do our best to explain
Our wishes. What happens?

Yesterday, I ended up
With gravy on my lettuce; and
Today, my wife got an ice in her tea.
And we shall be at sea

For five more weeks.

Some have children—
some have none.
Here lies the mother
of twenty-one.

Here lies the mother
of twenty-eight.
It might have been more
but now it's too late.

LOVE VERSES

The daffodils are growing;
Cut them with a knife.
If you want to marry,
Go and get a wife.

I love you a little, I love you a lot,
My love would fill a pan and a pot,
A bucket that's blue, a bottle that's green,
A basin, a bath, and a washing machine.

The old pig whistles,
And the little pigs dance;
All the girls are marrying,
But I can't get a chance.

TRUE LOVE

My love was a thousand miles away;
So I rang her up on Christmas day
(Which cost me more than half my pay).
    So full was my heart
    When I tried to start,
I couldn't think of a word to say.

HAIKUS

The Haiku is a Japanese form of poetry. In it the poet tries to give the essence of a mood—of something sad, or amusing, or surprising—all within three short lines. The first and third lines should have five syllables and the second line should have seven.

> A bitter morning:
> Sparrows sitting together
> Without any necks.
>
> J W Hackett

How happily she
laughs! on and on and on, a
waterfall of sound.

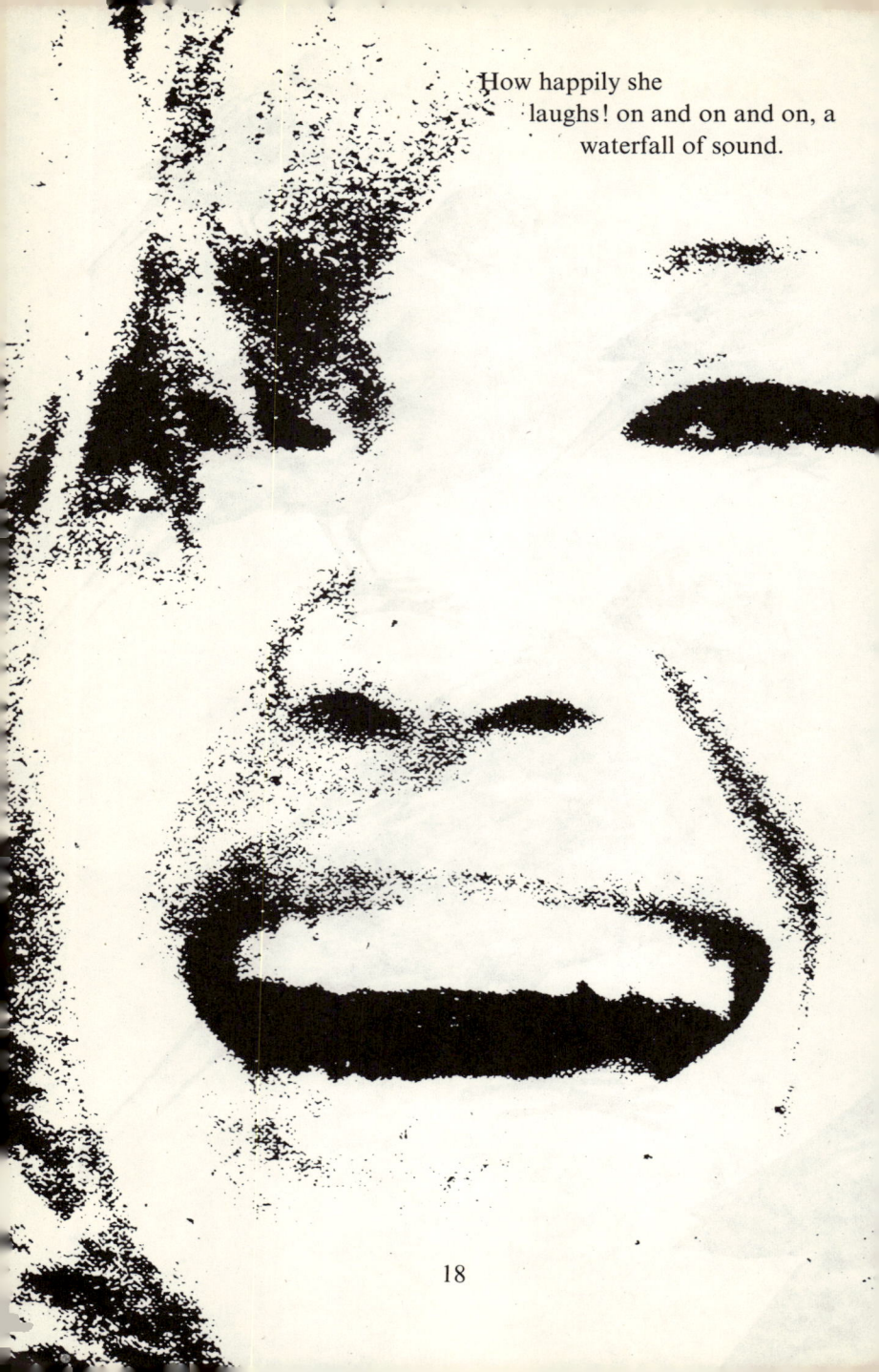

THERE IS NOTHING THAT IS NOT SPIRIT

'Explain more to me, father,' said Svetaketu.

'I will, my son.

Put this salt in water and come to me tomorrow morning.'

Svetaketu did as he was told. In the morning his father said to him: 'Bring me the salt you put into the water last night.'

Svetaketu looked into the water, but could not find the salt. It had gone.

His father said: 'Taste the water from this side. How is it?'

'It is salt.'

'Taste it from the middle. How is it?'

'It is salt.'

'Taste it from that side. How is it?'

'It is salt.'

'Look for the salt again and come again to me.'

The son did so, saying, 'I cannot see the salt. I only see water.'

His father said: 'In the same way, O my son, you cannot see the Spirit. But in truth he is here.

Everything in the world expresses that Spirit. That is Reality. That is Truth. *You are that.'*

from *The Upanishads*

LIMERICKS

There was a young man of Polzeath,
Who walked in the wind on the heath.
He opened his mouth
While facing the south,
And now he's without any teeth.

Nicholas Burns

A diner while dining at Crewe
Found quite a large mouse in his stew.
  Said the waiter, 'Don't shout
  And wave it about,
Or the rest will be wanting one too.'

'IT'LL SOON GO AWAY.'

A solitary churchyard, the sea and the moon.
The waves had broken up grave and stone;
A man was walking there, late and alone.

He saw a skeleton on the ground;
A ring on the skeleton's finger he found.

He went home to his wife and gave her the ring.
'O, where did you get it?' He said not a thing.

'It's the prettiest ring in the world,' she said,
As it gleamed on her finger. They went up to bed.

At midnight they woke. In the dark outside,
'Give me my ring!' a thin voice cried.

'What's that, dear husband? O, what does it say?'
'Don't worry, dear wife. It'll soon go away.'

'I'm coming. I'm now at the bedroom door.
Give me my ring! I'm crossing the floor.'

'What's that, dear husband? O, what does it say?'
'Don't worry, dear wife. It'll soon go away.'

'I'm coming nearer. I'm under the bed.'
The wife pulled the sheet right over her head.

'What's that, dear husband? O, what does it say?'
'Don't worry, dear wife. It'll soon go away.'

Then the sheet was snatched up into the air.
'I'm dragging you out of the bed by your hair!'

'What's that, dear husband? O, what does it say?'
'Throw the ring through the window! Quick, throw it away!'

She did so. They shivered with fear by the sill.
They heard dry bones clitter-clatter downhill,
Softer and softer... Then all was still.

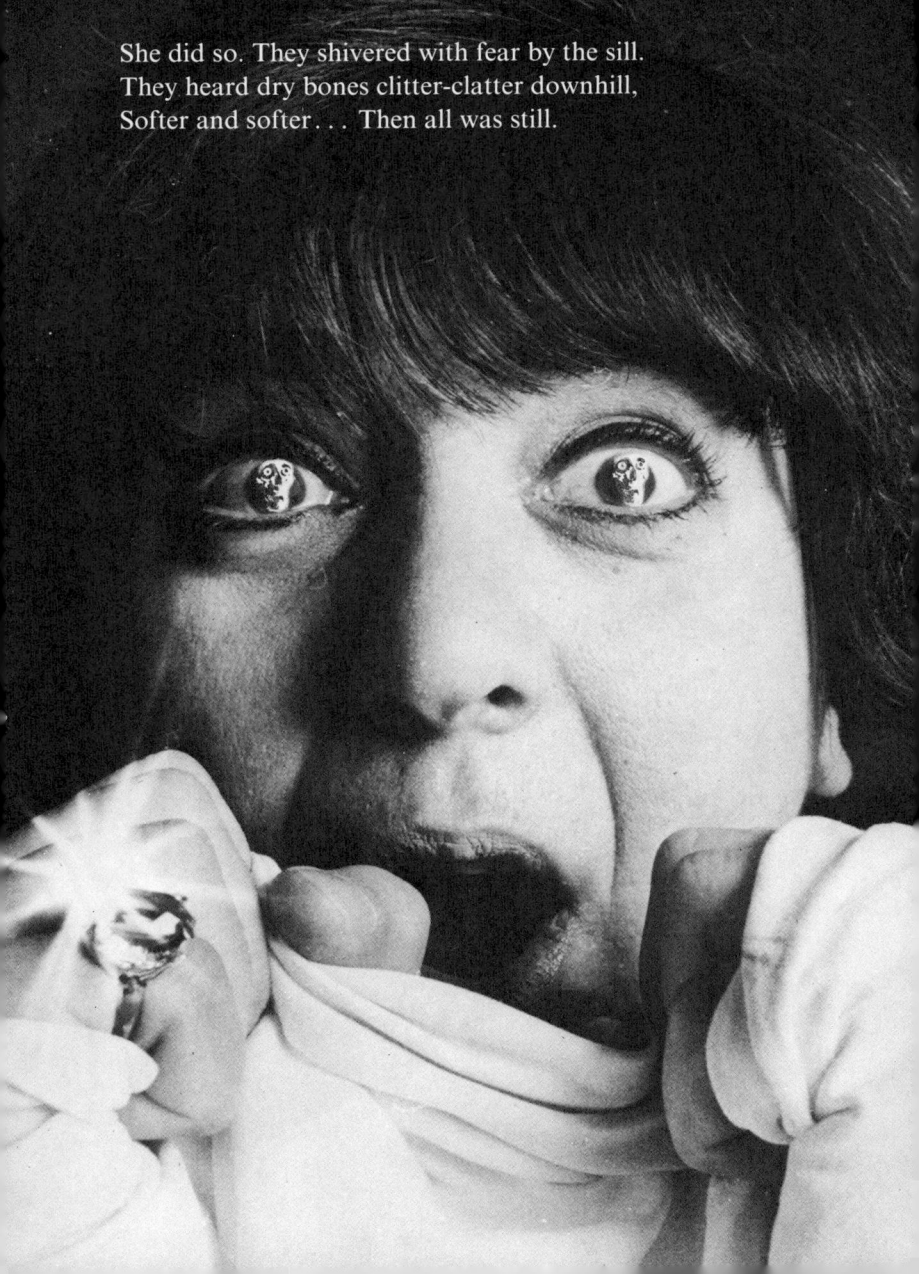

AN ACCIDENT HAPPENED TO JIM

An accident happened to Jim:
A boy threw tomatoes at him—
   Too soft, you'd suppose,
   To damage his nose,
But these were all packed in a tin.

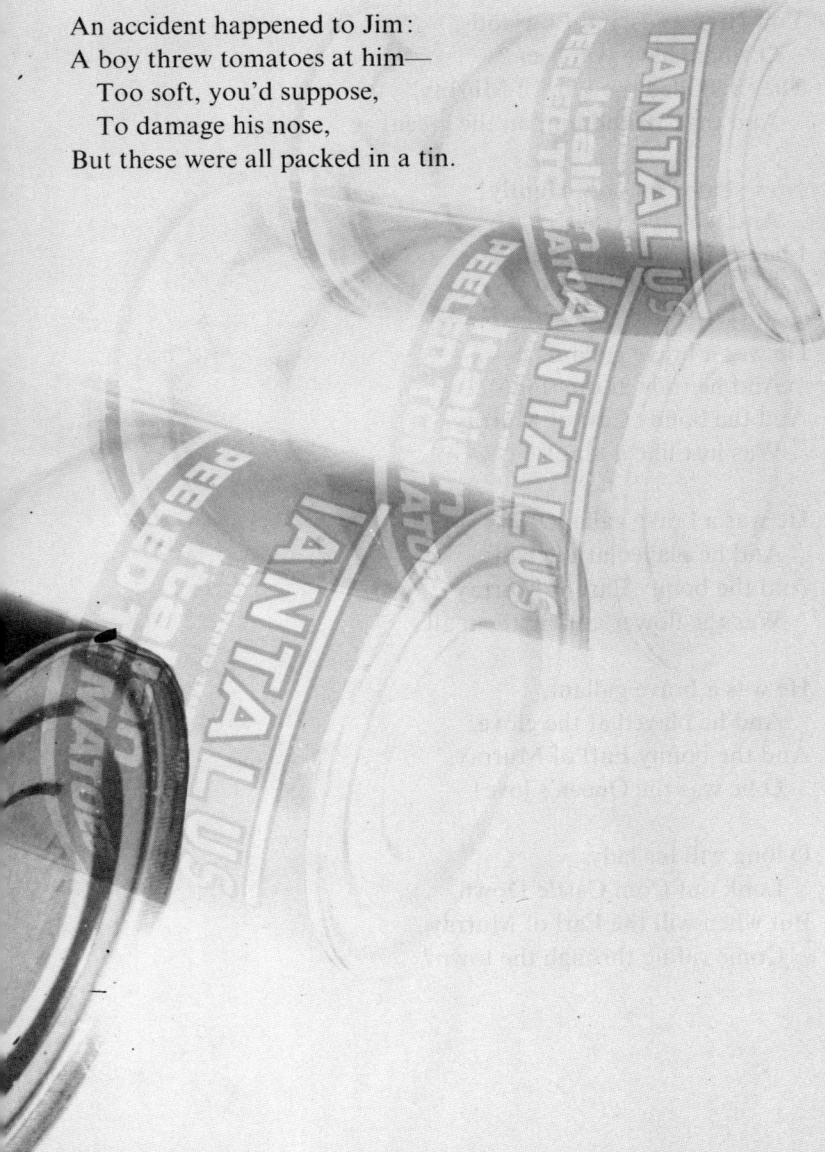

THE BONNY EARL OF MURRAY

You Highlands and Lowlands,
  O where have you been?
They've killed the Earl of Murray,
  And they've laid him on the green.

Now shame on you, Huntly!
  And why did you so?
I bade you bring him with you,
  As our friend and not our foe.

He was a brave gallant,
  And he rode at the ring;
And the bonny Earl of Murray,
  Was just like a king!

He was a brave gallant,
  And he played at the ball;
And the bonny Earl of Murray
  Was the flower among them all.

He was a brave gallant,
  And he played at the glove;
And the bonny Earl of Murray,
  O he was the Queen's love!

O long will his lady
  Look out from Castle Down,
But when will the Earl of Murray
  Come riding through the town?

TOO POLITE

Broad met Stout
At the gate, and each
Was too polite to brush past.
'After you!' said Broad.
'After you!' said Stout.
They got in a dither
And went through together
And both
        stuck
            fast.

PRINTED WITH FEET

For
your
comfort
over
the
stones,
the
Taylor
and
Bennett
families
have
made
this
path
of
sand

White sails, red sails
a seagull on the wave
a pool of sun
a swim

THE END

'My life is in ruins,
  I've come to the end.
It's time now to leave you;
  Goodbye, my dear friend.'

He swam out to sea
  Till we saw him no more.
Then a jellyfish stung him,—
  He swam back to shore.

Glossary

bade (pres. bid)	ordered: only used in poetry
bait	food put on the end of a fishing line
beast	animal
bind	tie
bitter	very cold
bonny	good-looking
brow	front of the head above the eyes
brush past	push past
come to pass	happen
crew	men working together, e.g. on a ship
damage	break, hurt or destroy
deceive	cause a person to believe what is untrue
delight	great pleasure
dew	water which forms on plants etc, after the sun goes down
distinguished	noticed by all, famous
dither	being very unsure and not able to decide
drag	pull a heavy object
express	say or show clearly
fast	firmly fixed
filter	instrument to take all solid or impure matter out of liquids
foe	enemy
forth; goes not forth	does not go out to sea
frequent	happening very often
gallant	good-looking young man
garland	circle of leaves or flowers
gleam	shine
glove	covering for the hand
gore	blood; only used in poetry
gravy	liquid from cooked meat mixed with flour.
heath	stretch of waste land
lettuce	vegetable with green leaves eaten uncooked.
lily	beautiful flower
mad *(drive me mad)*	make angry
mouse	small animal with a long tail found in houses
pig	fat animal used for food
pool	small hole in the ground with water in it
rat	animal like a mouse but larger
ruin	condition of complete loss or destruction
seagull	large sea bird
shepherd	one who takes care of sheep
shiver	shake with cold or fear
shower	slight fall of rain
snatch	take suddenly

sneeze	sudden outburst of breath through nose and mouth
spirit	soul, shadow-like form of a person supposed to be seen sometimes after death
spit	throw out (liquid) from the mouth
stew	meat and vegetables cooked in water
stretch	make larger or longer by pulling
stung (pres. sting)	prick the skin and drive in poison
thus	in this (that) manner
tomato	red fruit with salt-sweet taste
tower	tall building
wave (n)	up and down rolling movement on surface of water
weep	let fall tears, cry
whistle	make a high sound by drawing the lips together and blowing through them
yawn	opening the mouth wide as when tired or uninterested

Sources
Poems by Ian Serraillier

How cats began (adapted from a traditional poem)
On travelling from England to New Zealand
True love
It'll soon go away (adapted from a traditional ballad)
Too polite
Printed with feet
The end
How happily she laughs

Anonymous poems

Willie pushed his sister Nell
Young Sammy Watkins jumped out of bed
Willie with a thirst for gore
Six dukes went a-fishing (folk-song, adapted)
Early one morning
Weather
Epitaphs
Love verses
A diner while dining at Crewe
An accident happened to Jim
The bonny earl of Murray (old ballad, abapted)

Poems by other poets are acknowledged at the front of the book

Some titles in this series:
1. Recommended for use with children (aged 8–12)
2. Recommended for use with young people (aged 12–15)
3. Recommended for use with older people (aged 15 plus)
   No figure: recommended for use with all ages

Stage 4
The Prisoner of Zenda
Anthony Hope
Silas Marner
George Eliot (2.3)
The Thirty-Nine Steps
John Buchan
Seven Greek Tales
A.M. Nashif
Gold Robbery and Mine Mystery
Richard Musman (2.3)
The Angry Valley
Nigel Grimshaw (2.3)
Island of the Blue Dolphins
Scott O'Dell
The White Mountains
John Christopher (2.3)
The Birds and other short stories
Daphne du Maurier (2.3)
The Forger
Robert O'Neill (2.3)
Désirée, Wife of Marshal Bernadotte
Annemarie Selinko (2.3)
Fast Circuit
Bruce Carter

Plays
Three Mystery Plays
Donn Byrne
Loyalty
Richard Musman

Poetry
How Happily She Laughs and
  other poems
Ian Serraillier (2.3)

Non Fiction
Oil
Norman Wymer (2.3)

Adventure
Race to the South Pole
Lewis Jones and Bernard Brett

Stage 5
Kidnapped
R.L. Stevenson
The Adventures of Tom Sawyer
Mark Twain
The Sign of Indra
Nigel Grimshaw (2)
On the Beach
Nevil Shute (2.3)
Stranger Things Have Happened
Susan Bennett (2.3)
Mogul
John Elliot (2.3)
Bush Fire and Hurricane Paula
Richard Musman (2.3)
The Diamond as Big as the Ritz
and other stories
F. Scott Fitzgerald (2.3)
The Bike Racers
Bruce Carter (2.3)
Hard Times
Charles Dickens (2.3)
Désirée, Queen of Sweden
Annemarie Selinko (2.3)

Plays
The Seventh Key
Lewis Jones and Michael Smee (2.3)
Mystery on the Moor
Lewis Jones and Michael Smee (2.3)
Inspector Thackeray Investigates
Kenneth James and Lloyd Mullen
  (2.3)

Non Fiction
Animals Dangerous to Man
Richard Musman (2.3)
Man and Modern Science
Norman Wymer (2.3)